Believing While Grieving

A Journey to find Blessing in Brokenness

Bonnie Abadie

Balboa Press books may be ordered through booksellers or by contacting:

Balboa Press
A Division of Hay House
1663 Liberty Drive
Bloomington, IN 47403
www.balboapress.com
1 (877) 407-4847

Interior Graphics/Art Credit: Bonnie Abadie

ISBN: 978-1-9822-3578-9 (sc)
ISBN: 978-1-9822-3577-2 (e)

Library of Congress Control Number: 2019915270

Print information available on the last page.

Balboa Press rev. date: 09/30/2019

BALBOA.
PRESS
A DIVISION OF HAY HOUSE

Believing While Grieving

A Journey to find Blessing in Brokenness

Bonnie Lemelle Abadie

Foreword

This work began as my own private path through grief. I began writing things down with the thought that only my Spiritual Director and a few trusty souls with whom I would have the courage to share these thoughts would be the audience. I had no idea that the poems and my (fledgling) watercolor paintings would spark interest. It was my way of expressing the reality of my life, of working through the pain of loss and dealing with my new circumstances. But as I began to share these pieces, I heard the resounding call to "put this out there"!

While grief is personal, it is also communal and ultimately, it is a universal reality. I was told several times that these words and pictures may have the power to help others! So, in obedience to those who have encouraged, entreated, pleaded, prodded, and guided me, here is a sampling of my work!

Introduction

You may be saying, "Not another book on grief!" As long as humans deal with loss, then there will be tons of books on the subject. Yes, this is another book written by one who is working through grief, but I think you will find it to be different from other memoires or "how to" books.

In putting this before you, in no way am I trying to say that my grief is greater than what you may be suffering. In speaking my truth, I want to encourage you to explore the recesses of your heart, mind, soul and to creatively give voice to what is being brought to life inside of you at this moment. It is my sincere desire that you will find your story within what is shared here and that you will be assured that you are not alone.

The title: *Believing While Grieving: A Journey to Find Blessing in Brokenness*, captures the essence of my struggle. On the one hand, as a person of faith, I truly believe that my loved ones are with God, that the promises of the Resurrection are fulfilled through their new lives in Glory. I believe it with all my being and I celebrate and dance for joy at their complete union with God. I truly believe that I will see them again and that the best of them live on in all who knew and loved them. AND, at the same time, as a human being living my own "post-apocalyptic" existence, my family and I grieve the loss of Dad in 2013, and my Husband in January 2016 and Mom in October of 2016. It is a triple play of sadness, but my Husband is the real "star" of my grief show.

My Star: Maurice S. Abadie Jr. was born November 14, 1940 the second of four children of Helen Wilson and Maurice S. Abadie of New Orleans, Louisiana. At the age of 13 he entered the minor seminary run by the Congregation of the Most Holy Redeemer (the Redemptorists). He became a professed member of the Congregation of the Most Holy Redeemer in August of 1961 and was ordained to the Priesthood on June 22, 1966. Father Abadie served twelve years in active priesthood ministry. In the wake of the passing of his Mom in 1974 and his Dad in 1978, Father Abadie requested a leave of absence in order to discern his true Vocation. A romantic interest developed between us as we recognized each other as soul mates. I wanted him to be very sure that he wanted to marry me as a free person. When he was absolutely sure, he applied for a dispensation from the priesthood which was finally granted by Pope John Paul II in 1986. Maurice and I were married on June 13, 1987.

In life, one expects to bury parents, and the grief is still very real. The possibility of burying a spouse is 50-50. We did not have children, but I cannot even begin to imagine the journey through pain and loss that reality is for those who have buried a child. Loss is a part of life. Maurice was a "no excuses" kind of person and so most people were unaware of all the chronic diseases he battled. Surviving several near death experiences over a span of 16 years, he was a challenge to all of his physicians. Because his demeanor was always receptive if not 100% compliant, and he showed constant gratitude, many of them came to regard him as a special friend. I had the grace to be present with him as Maurice passed away peacefully on the morning of January 6, 2016. Maurice died between the two loves of his life: The Redemptorists through the presence of our pastor, Rev. Jim Shea CSsR and family represented by me.

The Journey: When I taught a course on Death and Dying back in the 1980's, we studied the stages set forth by Dr. Elisabeth Kubler-Ross as denial, anger, bargaining, depression and acceptance. Somehow, I had the thought that a person moves through these stages within six months to a year, and all is well, life resumes, happiness returns. Studying it and living it are two different things. I have discovered that the stages are not sequential, but spiral and cyclical. Time is not a factor.

The Struggle: Being a person of faith does not take away the human need to grieve. There is abundant loss: of the person, of identity in the survivor, of income and lifestyle, changes in civic and social status, changes in relationships to mention a few. The world turns upside down in many ways and no amount of denial, spiritualization or pretense can change this reality. There is a real sense of brokenness! Can one be in this space so as to discover God's presence? Can one find the blessing contained in this reality? I am discovering that it is possible to live in the blessing of grief. So as a person of faith, I resist being "guilted" into false happiness. In being true to the journey, I need to "feel what I feel when I feel it" and lean into the pain that will lead eventually to transformation and peace.

I think it is very important that we not short circuit the process by allowing well-meaning others to force open our cocoons or speed up the blossoming of the rose. There is plenty of hard work—physical, mental, spiritual, and emotional to be done before one can "move on", if that is even possible. We each have our own timetable for working through this reality and God is there. This is a journey into the Paschal Mystery wherein through our lives, suffering and death, we share in the life, suffering, death, resurrection and ascension of Christ our Lord. In our suffering, we touch the wounds of Christ from which pour gracious and generous healing for the life of the world. The journey leads us out of the tunnel of despair into the light where Resurrection is lived and celebrated every day.

About the work itself: Many of the words are poetic, but not intended to be poetry per se. There are glimpses of symmetry, meter, rhyme, alliteration, anagrams and other elements contained in poetry, but the point is to speak to a particular reality in such a way that the heart may capture and savor meaning. The accompanying art work came as a surprise to me. I always enjoyed Friday afternoon Art Class in elementary school. I have a brother and a niece who are "real artists" and I never considered that I might also have a gift. At the suggestion of a friend and colleague who gave me a set of watercolors, I decided to "see what you can do with these!" The photos were taken by me on my iphone.

Acknowledgements

First of all, I want to thank you, the reader, for picking up this work and taking it for whatever it may be worth for your life. If you are reading it, and it resounds within you, then I can only imagine that you may be going through some tough stuff right now. We may never meet in person, but as a Christian, I know you as a Brother or Sister in Christ. We are connected through our baptism into Christ. Together we are food for the hungers of the world through our unity in Him. And if you are not Christian, I know you as my Brother or Sister in the enterprise of humanity, sharing life together on this planet, breathing the same air, sharing the same resources, seeking love, compassion and understanding, searching for meaning in life especially through suffering and the pain of loss. I am offering this to you with a prayer for your healing, hope and comfort.

There are many other people to thank. First, I give praise and thanks to God, Creator, Redeemer and Inspirer for the gifts of life and love and for your Eternal Presence through every step of the journey. Next, I give thanks to my parents, August and Anna Mae for shaping, forming, loving me into existence, putting my feet firmly on the path of faith, and teaching me every good and every painful lesson about life. My siblings and their spouses: Patrick and Olivia, Jules, Allen and Mary, Angie and Tim (nieces and nephews too!) for your love, constant care and concern shown in many ways. My in-laws and their spouses: Johnnie and TJ, Yvonne, Rene and Cecelia (cousins, nieces and nephews too!) for your on-going loving relationships and for being instrumental (along with the Redemptorists) in shaping BC into the man with whom I fell in love and was privileged to walk. Speaking of that man, heartfelt, special thanks to Maurice (BC) for sharing my life, my heart, our home, for companioning me in mutual love, respect, friendship, hospitality, devotion, dedication, faithfulness, forgiveness, mercy, compassion, patience, generosity and so much more.

Special Thanks to Jeannette and Addie Lorraine for being most encouraging to "get this out there"; to my colleagues Fernando, Tina, Roger, Linda and Clyde for inspiring confidence in my artistic abilities; Rita, Donna, Theresa, Ana, Rose Mary, Sally, Carmen, Graciela, Margaret, Irma and Ron for allowing me to share my work with you while receiving your feedback. Thank you to Isaura for introducing me to the folks at Balboa Press, the folks at Balboa Press, and to Jim who reminded me to "keep it real". Thanks also to the "Wednesday Supper Club": Tom, Rita, Cherryl, Jamye, Ken, Kie, Leota, Catherine Ann and others for your interest, support and encouragement.

A profound thanks to all members and leaders of my parish, St. Gerard, San Antonio; certificate and degree programs students, staff and colleagues at Oblate School of Theology for all your love and support and for providing me with the "safe space to be broken for a while." For all these and so many more, I am truly grateful!

Bonnie Lemelle Abadie,
Fall, 2019

Dedicated to Maurice Sylvan Abadie Jr.
1940-2016
My best friend, true companion.
The "Skin Horse" who taught this "Velveteen Rabbit" what it means to become "real".

Poems from the Journey

Frightened

Frozen face, saucer sized eyeballs staring in the mirror

"What do I do now? How do I go on?"

The basics first: important papers, details and plans and phone calls

"If you need anything, let me know!"

How can I? I can't even think! I don't know what I need!

Frightened that I'll forget

Frightened I'll be forgotten

Frightened I'll be alone and abandoned

Frightened I'll die alone and unloved.

Fear is a terrible companion

Fear weaves its icy tentacles around my heart

    And holds captive the virtues most needed

Fear suffocates and forces me to breathe under water

Fear is the cloud that hides me from the sunlight

    And traps me, holding me hostage in darkness.

Love casts out fear! "BE NOT AFRAID,

I am with you to deliver you", says the Lord.

Reaching with trembling hands I grasp the essence of Love

And I am alive once more!

In the Fog

If I could lift the fog that inhabits my brain,

I could think

    And remember

        And understand

This great mystery of life!

But I am not in control of the weather

And so, I peer through the cloud

And hope for a ray of sunshine to guide me along the path!

If I could remove the claw

That is firmly clamped around my heart,

    I could laugh

        And dance

            With unlimited joy!

But I don't possess the tool that releases me

    From the steel trap of bereavement

And so, I walk woundedly

    Hoping someone will see my struggle

And offer compassion as strength for the journey.

If I could do anything at all,

I would peer into the window of windows of Heaven

    To see you at peace,

        Filled with joy

And surrounded by love

And I would be satisfied that life does have happy endings

And all things work for the good

For all those who love God.

And I would be in awe, still, and grateful!

May it be so!

Enter the Flame of Love

Red, orange, yellow, green, blue

The flicker and glow of my Lover's heart beckons me.

Filled with desire and pulsing with passion

I approach with caution and trembling.

What if I lose myself completely?

Will it hurt?

Will there be regret when the flame has consumed me?

Why am I reluctant to enter the heart of all being?

It is from there I came

In love, I was created

In love, I was formed

In love, I was born into this world

In love, I learned to relate to those around me as my circle grew wider

In love, I encountered the one who completed my soul!

I burned with the longing for union and still I stood back from the flame

Eight years of anxious waiting for the green light to appear,

standing on the edge of despair,

June 13, 1987 two hearts became one; two bodies became one person;

two souls became united at last.

Ah! The Flame of Love!

It melted, melded, purified, consumed, changed, transformed us both so that

When people saw one, they thought of the other.

Breathing, moving, praying, playing, arguing, living daily life, reconciling, loving, loving, loving

Being true to each other in good times and in bad,

In sickness and in health

Until Death do us part

Beyond Death do us part

One lifetime is not enough to live as lovers and friends!

Two hearts united but ripped apart; two bodies now residing only in one; two souls united in Christ throughout eternity.

My lover, companion, friend, soul mate has entered the Eternal Flame of Love. I watched him go; I asked for the Grace to let him go; I was consumed in his joy.

It is a wonder to behold through tear-filled eyes and jagged ragged heart holes,

The dance of color and heat and light; Creator, Redeemer, Sanctifier

Consuming my Lover; embracing him in the dance

Assuring me that Love remains

Tears make love grow,

Remember with gratitude our beautiful life!

Live well until it is time for me to fully

Enter the Eternal Flame of Love!

River

The Mighty Mississippi River ran by his house

Ran through his veins

The Mississippi was his cradle

    He was a "River Rat"

A river runs through San Antonio

    But to him it was a canal

The power of the Mighty River

    Formed and shaped him

He was a raging river for Justice,

    Equality, for the cause of the underdog

    For life for the Poor

His love was also a raging river rushing over me

    Washing away all doubt that we should be together

    For life

    For good

    For each other

    For God

His life of service was a raging river

    Speaking the Truth to Power

    Refusing "no" as a valid answer

Working tirelessly for quality education

Laughingly flowing over obstacles in his way

His diseases were a raging river too!

Coursing through his veins

Ruining his life

Making him ill

Making him weak and sad

Leading him to despair

Making him wonder if his life was worth anything at all?

"This is not the way things are supposed to be, Radar"

He would often say to me.

In the end, a river ran through him!

Filling his lungs

Surrounding his heart

Into his kidneys

He drowned in his waters of life.

The waters rage still! The river of sadness flows through me!

Dark, deep, mysterious, perilous, ferocious, abysmal

I drown in my river of tears!

A River now separates us

He safely on the other shore

And I securely on the opposite bank

Stung by the quick farewell

Stunned by the wide chasm

Suspended in awe at the power of the Mighty River

River of Life

River of Death

River of Life Eternal

Wash me and take away the pain!

Inundate me and bring me into your power

Before the Throne of God

Where waits my love for me

Ferrying me to the other side

Welcoming me Home into his loving embrace

For all eternity

Going with the flow

Let me flow into you and you into me

River of Life

River of Light

River of Love

River of Peace

Sorrow

From cloudy grey skies fall

    Drops large, small, soft and hard

They call me to see the dance of Sorrow

    Playing upon my memory

Sorrow for moments locked in the past

    Though forgiven, still haunt and taunt me

Sorrow for regrets unreconciled

    And tucked away in the baggage I carry

Sorrow for moments that cannot be right now,

    Yet seem real and true

Sorrow mostly for me now learning to live alongside you.

Sorrow—the seven swords piercing Mary's heart

    Touch my own

    Though childless, I nevertheless know pain of

    Sadness, worry, anger, indignation, embarrassment, loss and loneliness

Mary pondered all these things in her heart, the process allowed her to be

    Her truest self, fearless, free.

Sorrow, you are the school of life that fashions prophecies into promises,

    Promises into fulfillment

    No one escapes your reach

But with each touch there is Presence

    Revealing the heart of sorrow's depths
    Wherein resides JOY.

Solitude

Alone I came into this world,

Alone I will depart

Alone is where my soul resides

    Caught in the tides

    Between the shores of this and the afterlife

State of calm and unexpected Peace

I have found the place where

    Shadow and substance kiss

    Compassion and action collide

    Anguish and gratitude reside

In solitude, I glance the very presence of God!

I am by myself, but I am not alone,

Solitude provides a home

    In the center of the heart of being

    In the circle of life and the living

    In the Creator's very being

Rest child, be healed

Let my love be revealed

Breathe deeply the life of My Spirit

Drink of the nectar of renewal

Be filled

Be refreshed

Be satisfied

I have named every tear you've cried

Every word of distress sounded in my ear

In solitude, know my HEART

Be assured, I am always near!

Struggle

Like Jacob and the Angel locked in mortal combat
I fight with forces over which I cannot prevail
Sadness sits silently
Springing up surprisingly often
It will not obey my command to flee
It insists it has a constant home in me.

But appearances beckon me to throw off darkness
Show people I belong in the light
Nearly two years have passed, after all
"You are a strong woman of faith"
A model of how one should come through the pall

Ministers need to fix what is broken
So I need to appear to be "together"
I want to show others it is possible to move on
But my tires are all flat and forward movement is
    Slow and painful
Still, I paint my face with the expected smile
    And gun the engine another mile

Grief demands honesty

Suffering commands attention

Loneliness insists on waiting

Solitude forces encounter

Duplicitous living is not my style, yet I can find

    No safe place to just be broken for a while

Patience is in short supply

This is the essence of my struggle

21

Encounter With God

Me: So much on my mind
So many irons in the fire
Too many memories to embrace
Too many hurts to erase

God: I am the fire in your eyes
I am the desire of your heart
In you my confidence lies
I am your true home

Come and Heal!

Me: Weary past the bone
My very soul near coma
Rest does not refresh
I only grow older

God: Too long have you tended your own fires
You do not wait for help
Independent and isolated
You violate my communion

Come and Rest!

Me: I thirst!
But the water is like stone
It cannot be swallowed
Rock of ages? I choke.

God: Life is hard
Rocks are strong
Don't be surprised if water
Gushes out of one!

Come and See!

Me: The wind in the wilderness blows warmly
But I shiver at its roar.
Into the past I go wandering
Just to glimpse the ancient shore.

God: Look over your shoulder with gratitude
The past is held in my embrace
Entrust your heart's treasures to me
They survive and are safe

Come along now!

Me: Woman standing at the opening door
Invitation to step out of the dark room
Into the sunlit garden
I stand in the threshold frozen!

God: Gardens are for lovers
Lovers of creation
Lovers of nations
Lovers of beauty
Lovers of Love

Come and play!

Me: The garden is covered with ash
Tons of gray silt cover the landscape
The dust blocks out the light
Where and how am I to play?

God: The dust prepares a new day
Keep watch and you will see
For now, live in the ash
Know that I am there too!

Come and wait!

Me: In the waiting, a moment of Encounter
Freshness of a renewed Spirit Sparks
Alive my soul in the exchange
Love is the gift of Life itself!

God: Breathe in the breath of new life
Exhale the old, the tired, the stale.
Drink from the River of Refreshment
Feel yourself coming alive again!

Come Enjoy!

God is Near, God is Here!

Adrift upon a silent sea

My boat, the waves and me

Is it dawn or evening?

It's hard to tell which horizon I'm seeing!

But I know God is near

I know God is here!

Right now, there is calm

But soon, the winds may shift

And my boat may drift

and test my faith

Even if I capsize

God will find me in the wake

I see how far by grace I've come

I know the one guiding me home

So even when I fear

I trust God is near

Indeed, God is here!

I am not alone to be

Adrift upon a silent sea

My boat, the waves, my God and me.

Sweetness

Tender moments spent in the grasp of LOVE

Your Presence becomes palpable

Like Golden Sunlight at dawn's first trumpet

The rays of yellow, gold, orange against the

    Deep blue and turquoise backdrop

Paint promise for a peaceful new day.

I behold in wonder the colors swirling within me

    Calling forth a response of pure joy

Listen to the song of the birds! They sing what is written in my heart:

Sweet is this gift of life

Sweet are the memories of the past

Sweet is your Presence in my heart

Sweet are the people who surround me with love

Sweet is my desire to serve you

Sweet is my hope for healing and wholeness

Sweet is my time here on earth and precious

Like Ezekiel swallowing the scroll,

    The taste of honey is on my lips, running down my face,

    Everywhere in my mouth

I am bathed inside and out in your sweet passionate love

Thank you!

NEW

I feel something changing in me.

I don't know what exactly

It feels a little like Spring

But there's still the chill of Winter

My soul is turning and yearning for the Light

Soon I believe that all will turn 'round right.

My companions are still with me

They sit by my side and fill up my space

I swallow my pride:

I'm private and hiding the pain I own

Tired of wearying the people around

But Solitude, Silence and Suffering bring Grace.

There's something beginning to break through

    The cracks in my soul

God's working to mend and make me whole

It's hard to perceive but as true as the day

God's working a miracle in me today

Yes, God's working a miracle in me today!

Today there's still sorrow, but tomorrow I'll see

    The beautiful butterfly God's making of me

For now, I'll be patient, continue to wait

This New Creation from Heaven's Gate

Will be floating and flying, dodging and diving

Dreaming and scheming of what else will be.

Freedom

Finding the way out of the gilded cage

The songbird stands on the perch by the open door

Wondering what the wild world holds

Having memorized every contour of the bars that

    Have been "home", will anyone notice she has fled?

Wondering if the stirrings within are issuing change

Is freedom a state of mind?

A place in time?

Is this broken wing sufficiently healed?

Has time revealed the direction in which one will go?

A bird is not meant to be caged, her nature is flight

Step out, spread your wings, become airborne

Fly on the breeze, alight in the trees, test the currents,

Brave the velocity

Risk all to become your true self

When the Son makes you free, then you are truly free!

Free from fright and fracture

Free to embrace feeling, forgiveness, fortitude and freshness

Freedom to BE one's best possible self,

Fly, dear songbird,

Be free!

Bonnie-In-The-Box

Painted smile
A song not her own.

Bonnie-In-The-Box
Pop up with surprise
To bring laughter

Bonnie-In-The-Box
Be a good girl
Don't make waves
Don't make a splash!

Bonnie-In-The-Box
Can't be constrained
Look out!
She's emerging!

This is Me!

Emerging from the shadows

I fix my eyes toward the Light

Cold damp earth beneath my feet

Underneath my finger nails

    From scratching and clawing

    My way out of the cave in which I have chosen to dwell

But no more! No more subterranean existence!

I am a child of the Light!

I dwell above ground now

Strange as it seems, bright as the light that burns

But beings adjust for survival

I am set on revival

Out of the cavern of despair

    I search for hope

Out of the darkness of pain

    I search for wholeness

Out of the depths of anxiety

    I search for peace

Consumed by crazy busy life

    I choose to breathe!

Finite yet fresh,

This is me!

Begin Again

Rise while it is still dark
> And begin again to greet the light

When it dawns, there will be
> New vistas to be explored.

Greet things and people
> You've never seen before.

Begin again to believe
> God protects
> God guides
> God provides

Step out and greet the smell of grass so sweet
> With rain-kissed hope

Behold the fragile feel yielding
> To the contour of your shoes

And as you sing the Blues
> Remember there are other channels!

Begin again to receive
> God's blessings
> God's musings
> God's calling

Delight in the life you would love

God's Power is not just above

It is within you! Begin again!

Cicada Symphony

Underground for 17 years,

Arriving on the surface in the fullness of time

The cicada has one day in the sunlight!

How do they spend that time?

Worrying about a future they do not have?

Frantically gathering wealth for days not their own?

Leaving a legacy of fame?

They rub their magnificent wings together

    And provide music for all who will listen.

Sonic waves arising in the North

Moving rhythmically southward

Crescendo and decrescendo and silence

And begins again

Like waves breaking upon the shore

Or an arena full of sports fans

The wave moves

The symphony played

    For all who will notice

    For all who will listen

One great song of praise to the Creator

    For the one day above ground.

What is YOUR sound?

Seawall

Sitting on the Seawall in mid-morning calm

Seagulls mocking the frolic of fish in temporary flight

Boats sailing across the horizon

I keep my eyes on the North Shore

Though hidden from my sight, I know it is there.

Sitting on the seawall in the mid-morning sun

Her rays dancingly reveal the diamond sparkle of this beautiful treasure.

Playground for ducks, geese and cranes

And occasional dog-walking human

I listen for the cadence of the waves playfully hitting higher measures.

Sitting on the seawall in the mid-morning breeze

The storm clouds begin to gather

I would rather ignore the thunder roar of tropical clockwork predictability

Ginormous raindrops force me to flee

My lovely Pontchartrain seawall for now, the Lake won't miss me anyhow

The sturdy seawall endures.

45

Autumn is Returning

The changing of leaves from green to brown
The raking and mulching back into the ground
The smell of smoke from fireplaces around
Autumn is returning

Harvest Moon lighting the path
Feet in tandem fleeing the wrath of
Flying bats and yellow-eyed black cats
Autumn is returning

Abundant, rich food to fill our plates
As friends and family congregate
We pause in thanks with Table Grace
Autumn is returning

Our time to be born
Now my time to mourn
And miss you at every turn
Autumn is returning

Our favorite time of year
I face alone, but without fear
The landscape more beautiful through tears
Autumn is returning

Be Triumphant

A late winter walk in the woods reveal

    The trees are not dead

Behold the "ta-dah" of the redbud tree

Barren branches exploding in living color purple

Even the uprooted fallen tree

    Supports budding green shoots shouting,

    "And still, I rise!"

Be firm in your trust

    If God can do thus—

Can you dare to behold God's late winter presence in your soul?

God takes our tragedies and works them into

    Resurrection stories

God takes our sorrows and fashions them into

    Tales of wonder

God takes the dead wood of hearts grown cold

    And behold

The "ta-dah" of redbud blossoms

The budding green shoots in the fallen tree

In nature we can see—why not within me?

Let God work in silence

Be still

Be transformed

Be Triumphant!

49

Afterword

This has been just a small sampling of the creative expressions that have been blossoming since 2016. Thank you for accompanying me on this journey. In sharing these choice pieces with you, I hope that you have found a moment of peace and consolation. If nothing else, I hope you came to see that you are not alone in your personal journey through grief.

About the Author

Bonnie Lemelle Abadie is a native of San Antonio, Texas. Throughout her life in ministry (40+ years) in the Roman Catholic Church, she has served as a teacher, facilitator, retreat director, catechist, liturgist, youth and young adult minister, campus minister, spiritual director, formator, conference speaker and musician. She has recently become an award-winning poet and fledgling artist.

Printed in the United States
By Bookmasters